Dandelions and Daydreams

written by Margaret Hillert

illustrated by Judy Hand

Copyright © 1987 by Margaret Hillert
Library of Congress Catalog Card No. 86-63565
Published by The STANDARD PUBLISHING Company. Cincinnati, Ohio
Division of STANDEX INTERNATIONAL Corporation. Printed in U.S.A.

THE DANDELION

The dandelion that we know
Is found in many places.
Across the whole wide world it lifts
A million golden faces.
It grows in countries everywhere
And here at home in ours.
I think that it must surely be
God's favorite of all flowers.

BUTTONS

My coat is buttoned down the front
With buttons round and white.
The grass is fastened to the earth
With dandelions bright.
And God has buttoned up the sky
With little stars at night.

Zippers, which seem very clever,
Couldn't be as pretty ever!

STARS

When God has turned the day to night,
He sets the little stars alight,
And far above I see them glow.

I see some others here below
To light the dark that evening brings,
Small fireflies like stars with wings.

MY BACKYARD

My backyard is pretty small;
Just a patch of green is all,
One small tree that I can climb,
And flowers when it's summertime,
Sandbox in a spot of shade
With puppy dog and pail and spade.
God has made a happy place
In just a little bit of space.

EARS

Thank You, Lord, for ears to hear
Robins chirping songs of cheer,
Kitten's purr and puppy's bark
Mother's voice at early dark
Singing lullabies to me,
Soft winds through the maple tree,
Church bells ringing loud and clear.
Thank You, Lord, for ears to hear.

NOSES

Thank You, Lord, for noses, too,
That sniff small flowers wet with dew,
Smell the smells of Christmas pine,
Washing drying on the line,
Mother's fragrance in the night
When she comes to tuck me tight,
Chocolate cookies, homemade stew.
Thank You, Lord, for noses, too.

ABOUT FEET

The centipede is not complete
Unless he has one hundred feet.
Spiders must have eight for speed,
And six is what all insects need.
Other creatures by the score
Cannot do with less than four.
But two are quite enough, you know,
To take me where I want to go.
I'm glad that God has planned it so.

DAYDREAMS

I sometimes dream
Of things to see,
Of things to do,
And things to be.

God knows my thoughts,
My daydreams, too.
And with His help,
I'll make them true.

THE RAINBOW

I watched a rainbow through the rain,
Its colors showing very plain,
And I was happy, for I knew
That somewhere God was watching, too.

RAINBOW CATCHER

Rainbow color comes and goes
In the sprinkle of the hose,
Gold and green and pink and blue
Where the sunlight filters through.
In the spray that's gently blown
Is a rainbow all my own.
If I'm careful where I stand
I can catch it on my hand,
And rejoice to have a share
Of God's promise glowing there.

AT THE BEACH

I like to picnic at the beach.
The waves march up in rows.
I stand and let the little ones
Curl up between my toes.

I use a shell for digging sand
To make a castle high.
Sometimes I look for starry fish
Or watch the boats go by.

And when my mother fixes lunch
And spreads it on the rug,
She calls me to her side to get
A sandwich and a hug.

Before we eat we say a prayer
For God's good blessings everywhere.

PRAYER TIME

I fold my hands,
I close my eyes,
And say a little prayer.
This is the way
I talk to God,
And show Him that I care.

PRAYER

When you work and when you play,
Take a little time to pray.
At home, at school, or anywhere,
There's always time to say a prayer,
Even riding in a car.
God hears no matter where you are.
Prayer will keep Him close to you,
So talk to God in all you do.

LITTLE THINGS

I'm glad that God had Noah make
An ark so big that he could take
A pair of every beast and bird
And fish according to His Word,
For now our world is filled with things
Like butterflies with rainbow wings,
And yellow ducklings, small white mice,
A furry bunny, extra-nice,
A speckled toad upon a stone,
A kitten for my very own,
Small creatures meant for us to share
Since God has put them everywhere.

THE BIRTHDAY OF JESUS

You can't give a cake
With the candles aglow.
You can't give balloons
That are such fun to blow.
You can't give a present,
You can't give a card,
You can't give a party
And play in the yard.
So give Him your love
For as long as you live,
For love is the very best gift
You can give.

SING A SONG

Sing a song of Christmas,
Stars, and sleigh bells, too.
Sing a song of candy canes
And carols ever new.
Sing a song of angels
In choirs up above.
Sing a song of Christmas.
Sing a song of love.

WHILE WE SLEEP

The stars are shining in the sky,
And so my teddy bear and I
Have both been kissed and put to bed,
And now our prayers have all been said,
And soon our eyes will close up tight
While You keep watch throughout the
   night.